Native Americans

The Pomo

Barbara A. Gray-Kanatiiosh

ABDO Publishing Company

visit us at
www.abdopublishing.com

Published by ABDO Publishing Company, 8000 West 78th Street, Edina, Minnesota 55439. Copyright © 2002 Abdo Consulting Group, Inc. International copyrights reserved in all countries. No part of this book may be reproduced in any form without written permission from the publisher.

Printed in the United States of America, North Mankato, Minnesota.
012002 032011

Illustrations: David Kanietakeron Fadden
Interior Photos: Corbis, *Ukiah Daily Journal* (page 27)
Editors: Bob Italia, Tamara L. Britton, Kate A. Furlong, Kristin Van Cleaf
Art Direction & Maps: Neil Klinepier

Library of Congress Cataloging-in-Publication Data

Gray-Kanatiiosh, Barbara A., 1963-
   The Pomo / Barbara A. Gray-Kanatiiosh.
     p. cm. -- (Native Americans)
   Includes index.
   Summary: An introduction to the history and past and present social life and customs of the Pomo Indians, a tribe of northern California.
   ISBN 1-57765-600-8
   1. Pomo Indians--History--Juvenile literature. 2. Pomo Indians--Social life and customs--Juvenile literature. [1. Pomo Indians. 2. Indians of North America--California.]
   I. Title. II. Native Americans (Edina, Minn.)

E99.P65 G73 2002
979.4'0049757--dc21
                                             2001045892

About the Author: Barbara A. Gray-Kanatiiosh, JD

Barbara Gray-Kanatiiosh, JD, is an Akwesasne Mohawk. She has a Juris Doctorate from Arizona State University, where she was one of the first recipients of ASU's special certificate in Indian Law. She is currently pursuing a Ph.D. in Justice Studies at ASU and is focusing on Native American issues. Barbara works hard to educate children about Native Americans through her writing and Web site where children may ask questions and receive a written response about the Haudenosaunee culture. The Web site is: www.peace4turtleisland.org

Illustrator: David Kanietakeron Fadden

David Kanietakeron Fadden is a member of the Akwesasne Mohawk Wolf Clan. His work has appeared in publications such as *Akwesasne Notes, Indian Time*, and the *Northeast Indian Quarterly*. Examples of his work have also appeared in various publications of the Six Nations Indian Museum in Onchiota, NY. His work has also appeared in "How The West Was Lost: Always The Enemy," produced by Gannett Production, which appeared on the Discovery Channel. David's work has been exhibited in Albany, NY; the Lake Placid Center for the Arts; Centre Strathearn in Montreal, Quebec; North Country Community College in Saranac Lake, NY; Paul Smith's College in Paul Smiths, NY; and at the Unison Arts & Learning Center in New Paltz, NY.

Contents

Where They Lived 4
Society 6
Food 8
Homes 10
Clothing 12
Crafts 14
Family 16
Children 18
A Pomo Myth 20
War 22
Contact with Europeans 24
Elsie Allen 26
The Pomo Today 28
Glossary 30
Web Sites 31
Index 32

Where They Lived

The Pomo were originally made up of about 72 different tribes. They lived in small **bands** in present-day northern California. Their original homelands were bordered by other tribes and the Pacific Ocean.

The Pomo homelands were **diverse**. The land had mountains, rolling hills, and fertile valleys. The land also had redwood forests, and **stands** of pine, oak, and maple trees. Wetlands contained plants such as **tule** (TOO-lee) and willow trees.

Pomo bands lived along the Pacific coast. They lived in the valleys and along the lakes, rivers, and streams. Living along the coast meant the summers were warm, with moderate rain. The winters were mild with some rain, too.

The Pomo languages are from the Hokan language family. Each Pomo band spoke a different Pomo language.

The redwood forests of the Pomo homelands

5

Society

The Pomo lived in small villages. Each village had both male and female chiefs. Some Pomo groups passed down the chief title through inheritance. Other Pomo groups elected their chiefs.

The chiefs had to be respected by their people. They reminded the people of how to live in harmony with each other and the **environment**. They led activities, and arranged feasts and trade with other tribes.

The chiefs of each village chose a peacemaker to oversee trade. Trade was very important to the Pomo. If other tribes were unhappy with the Pomo, it could hurt trading. The peacemaker worked to create harmony between tribes. This allowed trade to continue without war.

The medicine people were also important. They healed sick people and conducted group ceremonies. Some medicine people used plants to heal. Others healed people through songs. Still others were given messages in their dreams on how to heal patients. It is said they could suck out illnesses. So they were called sucking doctors.

Special societies were also important to the Pomo. Some men and women belonged to sacred dance societies. The *Kuksu*, or Big Heads, was a **sacred** society for men. It was their duty to continue the traditional teachings of the tribe. They did rituals to keep the people healthy, and to ensure successful hunting, fishing, and gathering.

A Pomo village

Food

    The Pomo hunted, fished, and gathered their food. They hunted deer, elk, and pronghorn with bows and arrows. They used handwoven nets or snares to catch rabbits, squirrels, and birds.

    The Pomo also used bolas to hunt smaller animals. A bola had three to five long strings about three feet (1 m) long. A hunter tied the strings together at one end, and attached a rock to each of the other ends. The hunter swung the bola over his head and threw it. The animal became tangled in the strings, and was then killed.

    The Pomo fished in the lakes and rivers. They used spears to catch fish such as pike. To catch other fish, such as the sucker, the Pomo used cone-shaped willow baskets. The fish swam in the large end and got trapped in the basket. The Pomo also caught fish with nets and dams. They dried the fish not eaten right away. The dried fish could be traded or eaten during the winter.

    The Pomo gathered wild berries, roots, bulbs, buckeye nuts, acorns, grasses, and seeds. They gathered the seeds with special baskets called seed-beater baskets.

Acorns were also an important food. The Pomo hulled the acorns and pounded them into meal using a stone **mortar** and **pestle**. Then they poured water over the mush to remove its bitterness. They made the acorn meal into bread and mush.

A common Pomo meal was acorn mush served in a basket with dried fish. To make this, the Pomo filled baskets with water, fish, and acorn meal. Then they added hot rocks to the baskets. This made the water boil, which cooked the fish and mush.

A Pomo hunter using a bola

Homes

The Pomo built homes from materials found in their **environment**. Some Pomo lived in single-family homes. To make a house, the Pomo placed willow poles into the ground. Then they bent the poles and tied them together with vines to make a dome-shaped frame. They tied **tule** onto the frame to make the sides of the house.

Other Pomo built multi-family homes. These homes were about 40 feet (12 m) long. They housed a few related families. Each family slept next to their own fire and had their own door. They shared a storage area for firewood, a baking pit for cooking, and a **mortar** for grinding.

The Pomo tribes that lived near the redwood forests built dome-shaped homes from slabs of redwood bark. The homes were large enough to house extended families.

Each village had a sweat house. This small earth-covered building was constructed over a pit. Pomo poured water over hot rocks in the pit to make steam. The steam purified the body and relaxed the mind.

Larger villages also had earth-covered roundhouses. The Pomo performed ceremonies, songs, and dances inside these buildings. The societies also met in the roundhouses.

To build the roundhouse, they first dug a pit about 70 feet (21 m) around. Then they placed logs side by side to form a round frame. Small poles covered with earth and sod formed the roof. A smoke hole was left in the center.

Clothing

The Pomo made their clothing from natural materials. Women wove cloth from willow, redwood, and **tule**. They used bone needles to sew the plant-fiber cloth and animal skins into clothing.

Men and boys often went naked. When clothed, men wore kilts or **breechcloths** made from tule, buckskin, or rabbit fur. Sometimes they wore **leggings** and moccasins made from woven tule. The leggings and moccasins protected their legs and feet from thorns, branches, and sharp rocks.

Women wore long skirts that hung down to their ankles. They also wore handwoven mantles that tied at the neck. The mantles hung down to the top of the skirt.

In the winter, women wore extra animal skins beneath their skirts for warmth. Both men and women wore animal skin blankets in cold weather.

The Pomo wore special clothing for traditional ceremonies. Many men wore woven hair nets, feathered net robes, and feathered **sashes**. They wore earlobe decorations that they carved from wood, bone, and shell.

Men and women also wore headbands for special ceremonies. Men wore headbands made of woodpecker feathers and bird scalps. Women wore fur headbands decorated with hanging shell beads and pieces of abalone. Both men and women wore necklaces made from shells and bone.

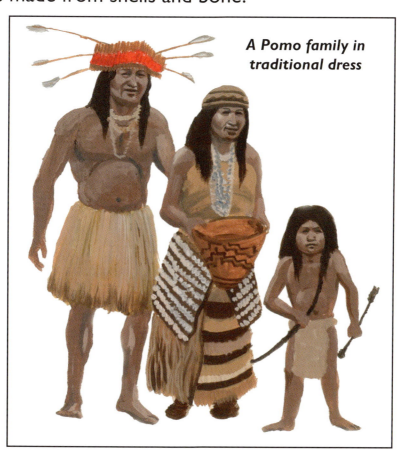

A Pomo family in traditional dress

Crafts

Pomo men used tall **tule** plants to make canoes. They harvested the tule from the nearby marshes. They bundled and tied it together with split grape vines to form the body of the canoe. When finished, a tule canoe was at least 10 feet (3 m) long.

The Pomo used beads for both decoration and trade. They made the beads from **magnesite** and clamshells. To make beads, the craftsperson baked pieces of magnesite and smoothed pieces of broken shells. Then they polished the beads and drilled them with a pump drill.

Pomo women were skilled basket makers. They wove baskets from willow, sedge root, and redbud bark. The Pomo used these baskets for everyday tasks, such as storage or cooking.

Pomo women were famous for their feathered baskets. They used a bone **awl** to make coils for these baskets. The women wove woodpecker and quail head-feathers into the baskets, covering the outside. They also wove **geometric** designs and shell beads into the baskets. These special baskets were given as gifts, or for personal protection. They were also used to heal the sick and honor the dead.

Each Pomo woman had her own basket-weaving materials. It was tradition to bury the woman's baskets and materials with her after she died.

Family

Family was important to the Pomo. They often lived in homes that included their grandparents, aunts, and uncles. Each person contributed to the survival of the people.

Men hunted and fished. They made tools such as knives and axes from chert and obsidian. They wove fishing nets and traps, and made **tule** canoes and bone hooks. Men also wove tule baby carriers.

Women gathered berries, nuts, and other plants. They prepared the food for daily meals and storage. They also made clothing and wove baskets.

Elders also had important roles. They hunted, fished, and gathered. They made baskets and beads. They also taught and helped raise the children. Elders often watched the children while the parents were busy with daily chores.

Men and women were free to choose their marriage partners. But their families had to agree on the choice. The families often gave gifts, such as feathered baskets, beads, food, and rabbit fur blankets. The Pomo prized marriages where the bride and groom spoke different Pomo languages. Speaking a different language allowed the Pomo to set up trade between the two villages.

Men used tule to make items such as canoes and baby carriers.

Children

Children were important to the Pomo. Babies were carried in willow baby baskets. They were bathed twice a day in a basket of warm water. Their diapers were made of woven **tule**.

Young girls often played with dolls made of tree bark. The dolls had shell eyes and wore willow skirts. The girls carried their dolls in small baby baskets. The elders showed the girls how to gather sedge, willow, and redbud to make the baskets.

Young boys practiced hunting by using small bows and arrows. They also played a game with rackets and balls. The racket had a webbed net on one end. The ball was made from a wood knot or deer knuckle. The object of the game was to carry or throw the ball through the opposing goal.

Elders taught children the history and traditional teachings of the Pomo people. They learned how to do special dances and sing special songs.

Pomo girls learned to weave baskets by making small baskets for their dolls.

A Pomo Myth

A long time ago, Coyote was angry with the people. He did not like the way the people treated his children. So Coyote decided he would get even by setting fire to the world. He rubbed his paws together and started a fire. But the fire surrounded and trapped Coyote and his children.

Suddenly, Spider dropped from the sky and saved Coyote and his children. Spider brought Coyote up into the sky. When the fire was out, Coyote came back down to the earth. He saw the burned land.

Coyote got very thirsty. He went to the river and drank water until he thought he would burst. A medicine man who had hidden from the fire came to Coyote. He tried to heal Coyote. The medicine man jumped on Coyote's stomach. Water began to pour from Coyote's mouth. It flowed and flowed. It flowed until the earth was completely flooded. This is how Coyote caused the great flood.

Coyote decides to get even by lighting the world on fire.

War

    The Pomo were a peaceful people. To prevent conflict or war, the village chiefs chose a peacemaker. The peacemaker's duty was to solve problems between the tribes in order to keep peace.

    Keeping peace meant the Pomo could continue to trade. Trading with other Pomo **bands** and tribes was important to Pomo survival. The Pomo had a highly developed trading system. They used strings of shell beads to trade for what they needed. The Pomo bought or traded shells, animal skins, feathers, basket materials, **Indian gold**, and food.

    If war became necessary, the war chief asked the tribe's trading partners to join forces against the enemy. The Pomo used spears with obsidian points. They used bows and arrows and a sling that shot clay pellets. For protection, the Pomo fighters wore body armor made from willow rods. The parallel willow rods stopped the arrows from hitting the body.

Pomo weapons: 1. Body armor 2. Bow and arrow 3. Feathered belt, used to confuse or scare the enemy 4. Spear

Contact with Europeans

In 1542, Juan Rodríguez Cabrillo sailed north along California's coast. During his expedition, he made trips to explore the shore. He claimed the land for Spain.

In the 1700s, the Spanish sent **missionaries** to California. Some Pomo living in the southern part of their territory were brought to the **missions**. Many Pomo converted to Christianity. The missionaries made them work on the missions. The Pomo were punished if they did not work.

Around 1800, Russian fur traders claimed land in California. They captured many Pomo people and used them as slaves. If the Pomo refused to work or tried to leave, the Russians killed them.

Around 1848, the California Gold Rush brought many new settlers to Pomo territory. The Pomo lost much of their land. In 1850, U.S. Army Captain Nathaniel Lyon led his troops to search for a group of Pomo who had killed white settlers.

Lyon did not find the escaped men. Instead, he attacked Pomo people who lived at Clear Lake. About 188 Pomo men, women, and children were killed. Today, this is remembered as the Bloody Island **Massacre**.

Since the Pomo first met Europeans, they have lost more than half of their population. The Europeans changed the Pomo way of life. They brought new diseases. The Pomo had no natural defenses to these diseases. They also died of starvation and poor treatment.

A Pomo man meets a Spanish missionary.

Elsie Allen

Elsie Allen was born in 1899. She was a famous Pomo basket maker. Many of her ancestors made baskets, too.

Allen learned how to make beautiful, traditional Pomo baskets from her grandmother. She also learned valuable **cultural** lessons as they made baskets. Allen learned where to gather plants. She learned to thank the plants for growing before she picked them.

Allen used her basket-making skills to help her people fight **racism**. In the 1930s, 1940s, and 1950s, Native Americans still faced racism. They were only allowed to sit in the back balcony of movie theaters. Their children could not attend public schools with white children. So Allen and other basket makers raised funds. The money went to college scholarships for Native Americans, to help Pomo people in need, and to fight racism.

Elsie Allen with her grandniece, Susan Billy

Allen taught basket-making classes for many years. She taught her grandniece, Susan Billy, the Pomo **culture** and weaving. Today, Susan Billy is a well-known basket maker. She continues the ways of her great-aunt, who died in 1990.

The Pomo Today

Around 1880, many Pomo raised money to buy back some of their lands, which had been taken by white settlers. Some men and women worked on ranches. Others wove baskets and sold them to collectors. With the money they earned, they bought back small pieces of their lands.

In the 1950s, the U.S. government created a policy of **termination**. This policy meant that the U.S. government no longer recognized the Pomo as a tribe. As a result, the Pomo lost their tribal rights and lands. Since then, the Pomo have fought many legal battles to regain their tribal status.

Some Pomo **bands** have had limited success in regaining their homelands. Some bands have been recognized again as part of the Pomo tribe. As a group, the Pomo bands received land for the *Ya-Ka-Ama* Indian Education Center. *Ya-Ka-Ama* means "Our Land" in the Pomo language. The center has many educational, **cultural**, and economic development programs.

Today, there are about 5,000 Pomo people. Some are lawyers or doctors who live in cities. Others live on small **rancherias** located on small parts of their original lands. Much of their land has been polluted by industry and other factors. They are working to protect sacred areas and wetlands that contain plants needed for healing and basket making.

Pomo people are working to preserve their languages and beliefs, and to strengthen their traditional ways. Many children are learning their people's stories, dances, and songs so their **culture** will continue into the future.

A river runs through Pomo traditional homelands in northern California.

Glossary

awl - a pointed tool for marking or making small holes in materials such as leather or wood.

band - a number of persons acting together; a subgroup of a tribe.

breechcloth - a piece of hide or cloth, usually worn by men, that is wrapped between the legs and tied with a belt around the waist.

culture - the customs, arts, and tools of a nation or people at a certain time.

diverse - composed of several distinct land forms.

environment - all the surroundings that affect the growth and well-being of a living thing.

geometric - made up of straight lines, circles, and other simple shapes.

Indian gold - magnesite beads, sometimes in strings, which could be used to trade for goods. Magnesite was highly valued by the Pomo.

leggings - coverings for the legs, usually made of cloth or leather.

magnesite - a naturally occurring silver-white mineral that contains magnesium.

massacre - the brutal killing of helpless or unresisting people or animals.

missionary - a person who spreads a church's religion.

mission - a center or headquarters for religious work.

mortar - a thick bowl in which substances are crushed into powder using a pestle.

pestle - a club-shaped tool used to pound or crush something.

racism - a belief that one race is better than another.
rancheria - a tract of land reserved for Native Americans use. It is usually a smaller portion of the tribe's original homelands.
sacred - having to do with religion.
sash - a band of material worn about the waist or over one shoulder.
stand - a group of trees.
terminate - to come to or bring something to an end.
tule - a reed that grows in wetlands.

Web Sites

Elem Pomo History
http://www.elemnation.com/
Visitors can read about the history and culture of the Elem Pomo village.

Elsie Allen
http://www.kstrom.net/isk/art/basket/elsieall.html
This site includes a biography of Elsie Allen along with information about traditional Pomo baskets.

These sites are subject to change. Go to your favorite search engine and type in Pomo for more sites.

Index

A
Allen, Elsie 26, 27

B
baskets 8, 9, 14, 15, 16, 18, 22, 26, 27, 28, 29
beads 14, 15, 16, 22,
Billy, Susan 27
Bloody Island Massacre 25

C
Cabrillo, Juan Rodríguez 24
California Gold Rush 24
canoes 14, 16
ceremonies 6, 11, 12, 13
chiefs 6, 22
children 12, 16, 18, 25, 26, 29
Christianity 24
clothing 12, 13, 16
crafts 14, 15, 26, 27

D
dances 7, 11, 18, 29
diseases 25
dolls 18

E
elders 16, 18

F
family 10, 16, 17
fishing 7, 8, 16
food 8, 9, 16, 22

G
games 18
gathering 7, 8, 16, 18, 26

H
history 18
homelands 4, 24, 28, 29
homes 10, 11, 16
hunting 7, 8, 16, 18

J
jewelry 13

L
languages 4, 17, 29
Lyon, Captain Nathaniel 24

M
marriage 16, 17
medicine people 6, 7, 20
missionaries 24
myth 20

P
peacemaker 6, 22

R
rancherias 29
rituals 7, 10
roundhouse 11
Russians 24

S
slavery 24
societies 7, 11
songs 6, 11, 18, 29
Spanish 24

T
trade 6, 14, 17, 22, 24
tribes 4, 6, 10, 22, 28

U
U.S. Army 24
U.S. government 28

V
villages 6, 10, 11, 17, 22

W
war 6, 22
weapons 8, 18, 22

Y
Ya-Ka-Ama Indian Education Center 28